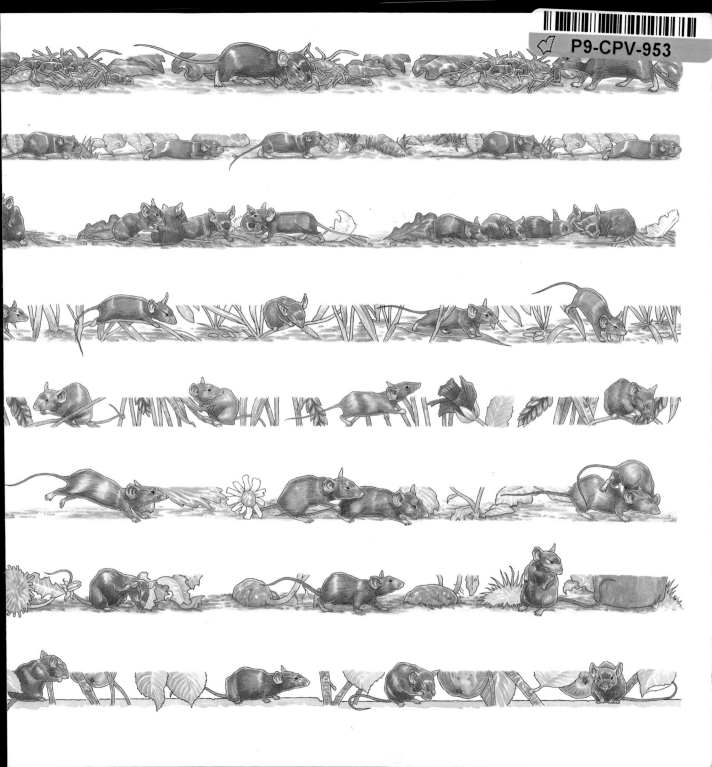

A DORLING KINDERSLEY BOOK

Canadian Cataloguing-in-Publication Data

Royston, Angela
  Mouse

(See how they grow)
ISBN 0–590–73866–6

1. Mice – Infancy – Juvenile literature.2. Mice –
Development – Juvenile literature. 3. Mice
Juvenile literature. I. Watts, Barrie. II . Title.
III. Series: Royston, Angela. See how they grow.

QL737.R666R68 1992   j599.32'33   C91–095242–6

First published in Canada in 1992 by Scholastic Canada Ltd.
123 Newkirk Road, Richmond Hill, Ontario, L4C 3G5.

Originally published in Great Britain in 1992 by
Dorling Kindersley Limited, 9 Henrietta Street, London WC2E 8PS

Printed in Italy by L.E.G.O.   ISBN 0–590–73866–6

Written by Angela Royston
Editor Mary Ling
Art Editor Nigel Hazle
Production Louise Barrett
Illustrator Rowan Clifford

Color reproduction by J. Process Ltd, Singapore

SEE HOW THEY GROW
MOUSE

photographed by
BARRIE WATTS

Scholastic Canada Ltd

Just arrived

I have just been born.
I cannot see or hear.
I have no fur to
keep me warm.

I snuggle in a
cozy nest with my
brothers and sisters.

This is me

This is our mother. She is
coming to feed us her milk.
We are very hungry.

Out of the nest

I am two days old. Fine black
hair is growing over my pink skin.
My eyes and ears are still closed.

Where am I?
I am lost!

I squeak as loud as I can so Mother hears me. She will carry me home.

My first crawl

I am two weeks old. My eyes
are open. At last I can see
and hear. I can walk too.

My mother watches me explore.
I sniff everything I find.

Now I am going back to my nest for a nap. It has been an exciting day.

Playing in a flowerpot

I am three weeks old. My claws are sharp, and my legs are getting strong.

I like playing in this flowerpot.
But the walls are slippery.
Help! The pot is rolling away.

From here,
I can see
all around
my world.

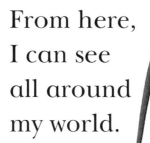

Look! My sister is
peeping out of
another flowerpot.

Looking after ourselves

Now I am four weeks old.
I spend most of the
time with my brothers and sisters.

We play together.

Then I clean
myself. My
long tail needs
special care.

Climbing high

I am six weeks old.
My brothers, sisters,
and I have climbed
this branch.

We cling to the thin
branches with our claws.

Our long tails
help us to balance.

Finding food

Now I am eight
weeks old. I enjoy finding
my own food.

I sniff and
twitch my nose
when I smell
something
good to eat.

My favorite food is grain. I hold it between my paws and nibble it with my long front teeth.

See how I grew

Newborn

Two days old

Two weeks old

Three weeks old

Four weeks old

Six weeks old

Eight weeks old

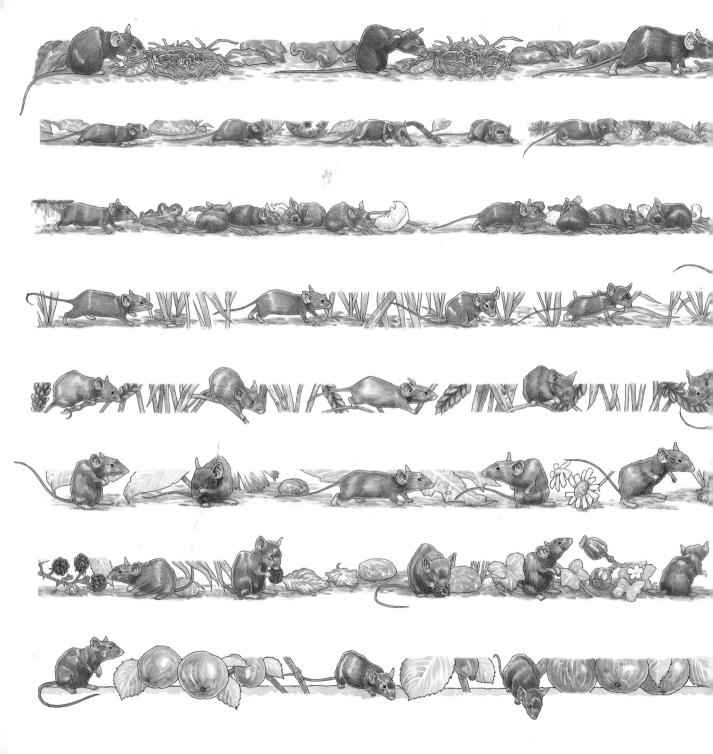